You might as well be dead

A catalogue of frightening facts

First published in 2008
by Oldie Publications Ltd
65 Newman Street, London W1T 3EG
www.theoldie.co.uk

ISBN-10: 0954817672
ISBN-13: 978-0954817671

A catalogue record for this book
is available from the British Library

Printed by CPI Cox & Wyman

YOU MIGHT AS WELL BE DEAD

Richard Ingrams
With illustrations by Martin Honeysett

Oldie Publications

Warning. Reading is a hazardous activity. Proceed with caution.

Introduction

In recent years the press and television have become altogether more aware of their duties to keep the public abreast of the latest findings of medical researchers.

News bulletins regularly report the advances made by doctors in discovering links between disease and various foods, drinks or some activity which had hitherto been thought of as reasonably harmless. At the same time, newspapers have in many cases instituted regular columns to warn their readers of a variety of risks.

Such is the plethora of research in this area that I feel sure many people have failed to make a note of all the health hazards that have been brought to light by medical pioneers.

For this reason, I have long thought it would be helpful if the essential information were made available to the public in a handy and easily comprehensible form.

I hope that this book will provide the answer. It could be, however, that readers may conclude that the game is not worth the candle and in a spirit of irresponsibility and recklessness avoid taking any necessary health precautions. Such a response would, I suggest, be foolish and immature.

Richard Ingrams.

Air Fresheners

Writing in the *Medical Science Monitor* Dr Richard Lawson warns that the innocent looking air freshener in the toilet can cause anxiety, insomnia and palpitations.

The Week (19/10/96)

Airports

A study from the Chartered Society of Physiotherapy revealed that most English airports do not meet EU-recommended limits on the pollutant gas, nitrogen dioxide. The gas can cause asthma, bronchitis and emphysema.

BBC News (13/03/06)

Air Travel

Plane journeys as short as three to four hours can be dangerous, doctors warn. The cramped seating causes dangerous blood clots in the legs which can have fatal consequences.

Independent (26/08/88)

Alarm Clocks

A Japanese study found that those forced awake from alarm clocks had higher blood pressure and heart rates than those who woke up naturally.

Daily Mail (24/10/06)

Aspirin

Did you know that aspirin – still the most widely-used non-prescription painkiller – can have some serious side-effects? It may make you deaf, destroy valuable vitamins, give you stomach ulcers and affect the kidneys.

Mail on Sunday (18/11/84)

In April 1985, Dr Andrew Forge, a lecturer at the Institute of Laryngology and Otology, London University, claimed that 500,000 people had had their hearing severely damaged by commonly-used medicines.

Daily Telegraph (19/4/85)

Bacon

Bacon is highly dangerous, say researchers at the Columbia University Medical Center in New York. Eating it regularly doubles the risk of developing chronic lung disease, they warn.

Daily Mail (14/4/07)

Baths and Showers

In August 1986 the *New Scientist* reported the findings of Julian Andleman, Professor of Water Chemistry at Pittsburgh University.

The professor concluded that taking long hot showers was a health risk and that relaxing in a hot bath was only marginally less dangerous.

Hot showers, said the report, cause poisonous chemicals evaporating out of the body to be inhaled.
Daily Telegraph (18/9/86)

Taking a bath immediately after a meal can be especially hazardous. In November 1987 a teenage judo champion, Mark Duckett of Locks Heath, Hants, died in a bath only minutes after eating a burgers and beans supper. Said the coroner, Mr Michael Baker: 'This is a good example of the dangers in having a bath after a meal.'
Guardian (13/11/87)
See also **soap**

Beef
Infertility in men could be caused by their mothers eating too much beef during pregnancy, according to the *American Journal of Human Reproduction*.
Metro (28/03/07)

Beer
Drinking seven pints of beeer a week can make your brain shrink, according to researchers at Wellesley College in Massachusetts. Shrinkage of the brain increases the risk of epileptic fits, they added.
Daily Mail (03/05/07)

Bicycles

Sitting on a hard bicycle seat can lead to sexual problems for both men and women, says professor Irwin Goldstein of Boston University School of Medicine. Male cyclists are more liable to suffer from 'changes in ejaculatory sensation, difficulty in urinating, and chronic numbness and pain.'
Women run the risk of clitoral pain and trouble in achieving orgasm.
The Week (20/06/98)

Binge drinking

A Northumbria University psychologist, Dr Thomas Heffernan, warns that teenagers who binge drink risk brain damage and premature loss of memory.
Daily Mail (04/04/08)

Blackberries

Blackberries near busy main roads have been found to contain five times the safe limit of lead, a neuro-toxin absorbed from exhaust fumes, which can cause brain damage in children.
Daily Telegraph (08/09/89)

Bleach

If you bleach your undies – even cotton ones – the elastic in the waistbands of knickers and in bra straps is chemically altered and can cause a nasty skin irritation.

Mail on Sunday (18/11/84)

Boiled Eggs

Scientists at the Center for Disease Control in Atlanta, Georgia, have discovered that the soft-boiled egg is a health hazard.

The reason is the salmonella bacterium which can penetrate the yolk of an egg. The scientists advise that those foolhardy enough to eat a boiled egg should boil it for at least seven minutes if they are to avoid the risk of salmonella poisoning.

Independent (15/04/88)

Bracken

Bracken may look like a harmless enough plant as you wade through it on moor and mountainside.

But many scientists now believe that bracken is a killer which can cause cancer.

Professor Jim Taylor of the University of Wales in Aberystwyth has said, 'I regard bracken as a present-day triffid. I see no way of controlling it before the end of the century... It affects animals and there is no recovery. It causes cancer of the mouth, throat, gut and stomach.'

Sunday Telegraph (15/11/87)

Cannabis

It is a mistake to think that cannabis is a safer
alternative to nicotine or alcohol.

A United Nations consultant on Narcotics, Professor
Gabriel Nahas, spent fifteen years researching
cannabis abuse, concluding that 'it can completely
change the personality and lifestyle of the user ...
impair short-term memory and learning, male
fertility, female ovulation, pre-natal development, the
immune system and the heart and lungs.'
Daily Mail (03/11/83)

Eighty per cent of patients diagnosed with
schizophrenia are heavy users of cannabis, says
psychiatrist Professor Peter Jones of Cambridge
University.
   An American study found that smoking just half
a cannabis joint could trigger schizophrenia-related
symptoms.
Daily Mail (29/01/07)

Carpets

Fitted carpets harbour alarmingly high levels of
pesticides, heavy metals and polychlorinated bi-
phenyls, says John Roberts, an environmental
engineer from Seattle.
The Week (22/12/01)

Cars

Car drivers breathe in three times as much toxic gas as cyclists and pedestrians, say researchers at the Institute of European Environment Policy. They are at risk from carbon monoxide, nitrogen dioxide, soot particulates and benzenes which have been implicated in cancer and heart disease.

The Week (06/12/97)

Celery

A little-read organ, *Archives of Dermatology*, alerted American readers to the dangers of this harmless-seeming vegetable.

It was found that workers at an Oregon supermarket seemed to suffer from sunburn after touching cut celery. A condition known as phytophotodermatitis results from substances called psoralens, which occur naturally in celery.

Independent (17/11/87)

Central Heating

Germs, skin problems, poor concentration and lethargy – these are only a few of the dangers involved in heating your home. Researchers at the University of East Anglia also warn of the higher rates of eczema that can result from turning the heating up.

Daily Mail (26/12/07)

Chewing Gum

A sweetener used in sugar-free chewing gum could be a health risk.

Scientists at Berlin University have claimed that sorbitol (also known as E420) can cause severe weight loss, abdominal pain and diarrhoea.

Daily Mail (11/01/08)

Christmas

An American psychologist, Dr Richard Rake, has drawn attention to the tension which results when people contrast their own Christmas with the good time which they think everyone else is having.

Dr Rake quantified the stress and concluded that the average family Christmas rated 'somewhere between taking out a mortgage and having a minor run-in with the police.'

The Times (12/12/84)

A Norwegian scientist, Mr Arne Fjellberg, has claimed that the average Christmas tree has about 30,000 bugs and insects in it.

A microscopic investigation revealed midges, fleas, lice, parasitic wasps, spiders and beetles.

Guardian (21/12/84)

Some people can be allergic to Christmas trees. The *British Medical Journal* (1987) reported the case of a Liverpool woman who suffered severe eczema on her hands and face after buying a 'strong-smelling' Christmas tree. This was caused by an allergic reaction to colophony (rosin) which is also found in turpentine, varnishes, furniture polish and adhesive tape.

Independent (22/12/87)

In December 1987, Dr John Emslie of Scotland's Communicable Diseases Unit warned that 'kissing under the mistletoe can spread diseases'.

Daily Telegraph (23/12/87)

Coffee and Tea

Both of these popular beverages are highly dangerous.

Coffee

Can be dangerous, according to researchers at University College, Swansea, because it increases euphoria 'or the sense of happiness' in those who have drunk too much. An excessive amount of coffee can impair performance and increase reaction time.

Daily Telegraph (08/11/83)

A Norwegian report published in March 1985 concluded that coffee may increase the risk of heart attacks.

Daily Telegraph (25/03/85)

Tea

Two surgeons at Manchester University, Mr Rory
McIlroy and Mr Robert Pearson, spent six months
researching the tea peril.

They concluded that a steaming cup of tea can
contribute to ulcers.

Daily Telegraph (25/08/86)

Commuting

The European Foundation for the Improvement of
Living Conditions issued a report in 1985 drawing
attention to the damage involved in commuting.

Amongst the effects, said the report, were
headaches, chest pains and palpitations.

The Foundation claimed that 'travelling to
and from work can contribute to everything from
sleeplessness and digestive disorders to skin
complaints and excessive perspiration.'

Daily Telegraph (11/03/85)

Computers

A psychiatrist, Dr Prem Misra, has warned that
teenagers can become seriously disturbed when they
allow computers to take over their lives. 'They suffer
nightmares, illusions, excessive daydreaming and
exhaustion,' he said.

Daily Mail (02/09/85)

Eight hours or more a day spent in front of a computer screen is linked to glaucoma, one of the leading causes of blindness.

Daily Mail (26/12/07)

Computer games

Dr John Charlton, a psychologist at Bolton University, has made a study of players of computer games and warns that the games may become addictive. Those affected are likely to display low self-esteem and introverted behaviour – known to be symptoms of autism.

Daily Mail (03/04/08)

Computer Printers

Australian scientists have warned that at least a third of computer printers produce high concentrations of ultra-fine dust which can increase the risks of lung and heart disease, strokes and cancer.

Daily Mail (01/08/07)

Condoms

Some American condoms have been branded as a health hazard. Researchers from the Bronx discovered that condoms had been dusted with lycopodium powder to prevent them sticking to one another. The powder consists of the staghorn clubmoss (Lycopodium clavatum) which can cause allergic reactions ranging from dermatitis to asthma.

Writing in *Nature*, Michael Balick and Joseph Beitel warned that 'of most concern are reports of lycopodium spores causing adhesions on serous tissues and foreign-body granulomas in soft tissues'. However, the writers reassured patients: 'These granulomas are non-lethal, do not lead to cancer and are easily remedied. This is a relatively minor health problem compared with AIDS.'

Independent (18/04/88)

(See also **sex**)

Credit Cards

The humble credit card can constitute a health hazard, according to a report in the *London Evening Standard*. If carried in the hip pocket, cards can give rise to pain in the backside. The condition is known to the medical profession as 'credit card sciatica'.

(01/11/83)

Dancing

Dr Philip Radford and Dr Robert Greatorex of Cambridge have identified a condition called 'jazz ballet bottom'. The condition affects those who frequently spin round on their bottoms.

The movement, combined with the concentration of body weight on the base of the spine, gives rise to painful abscesses and may have to be treated with an operation.

Daily Telegraph (28/12/87)

Deck Chairs

A survey published in October 1987 by the
Consumers Association revealed that at least 2,500
people per annum need treatment after being pinched
or wrenched by garden deck chairs, described in the
survey as a 'particularly perverse' type of furniture.
Guardian (22/10/87)

Delia Smith

Professor Graham MacGregor of the St George's
Hospital Medical School has accused Delia Smith of
putting people's health at risk by using too much salt
in recipes.
Metro (07/04/08)

Desks

A team at the University of Arizona found that the
average office desktop harbours 400 times more
bacteria than the average office toilet seat.

Women's desks tend to harbour far more germs
than men's, they warned.
BBC News (16/02/07)

Dieting

A report published by the Committee on Medical
Aspects of Food Policy (Coma) has warned that crash
dieting may be harmful to health.

The report stated: 'Serious risks to health are associated with the use of very low-calorie diet preparations containing substantial proportions of low-quality protein or inadequate quantities of minerals or micronutrients.'

The Committee also questioned whether prolonged dieting conveyed any benefit, arguing that use of crash diets may lead to loss of non-fat (muscle) tissue which would make it more difficult to maintain slimness in the long run.

Independent (19/12/87)

Dr John Blundell of Leeds University has claimed that dieting is linked with mental illness. Said the Professor: 'Dieting is not innocuous behaviour. Physiological changes occur, including alteration to the balance of neurochemicals.'

The Times (19/04/88)

Dr James LeFanu of the *Daily Telegraph* revealed that a study of 6,000 Frenchmen on low-cholesterol diets showed they were twice as likely to commit suicide as non-dieters.

The Week (05/10/96)

Divorce

The stresses of marriage are well-known but 'splitting up' will not necessarily make things better.

In March 1984 Mr Jack Dominian of the Marriage

Research Centre informed the Royal College of Physicians that divorce entailed not only psychological problems but also led to greater symptoms of physical illness, such as heart disease and high blood pressure.

Dr Dominian also claimed that divorced and separated people had a higher mortality rate and became more ill more frequently than the single and married.

Daily Telegraph (29/03/84)

Scientists at the Common Cold Research Unit in Salisbury, Wilts, have discovered a link between divorce and the common cold. The Unit's director, Dr David Tyrrell, said: 'Stress of various sorts makes you more vulnerable to catching a cold, especially stress involving a distinct change of circumstances whether good or bad.'

Daily Telegraph (14/09/87)

Women whose loved ones are going away, or whose parents have died or left them, frequently suffer acute vulval irritation.

The Times

Doormats

Bristol City Council has threatened to remove doormats from council houses because they pose 'a tripping hazard'.

Guardian (14/09/06)

Drink

Most readers probably know that if you drink too much it affects your liver. But other consequences are perhaps not so well known.

In addition to damage to the brain, nervous system or liver, heavy drinking has been associated with high blood pressure, heart disease, obesity, vitamin deficiency, stomach ulcers and cancer of the mouth, throat and liver.
The Times (04/10/84)

A Japanese report published in March 1984 warned that men who drink more than a can and a half of alcohol a day are three times more likely to get cancer of the rectum than non-drinkers. This was the conclusion of a fourteen-year-old study of the relationship between cancer and alcohol.

A survey of more than 8,000 Japanese men also showed a link between whisky and wine drinking and lung cancer.
Daily Telegraph (09/03/84)

An alarming report published by the Royal College of Physicians in April 1987 warned of the startling effects that drink could have on the bodies of men and women.
　　The report claimed that drink causes men to grow breasts and women to become 'more manly'. Besides growing breasts, the Royal College warned, 'men can lose body hair and suffer shrinking of the sex organ.'
Daily Mail (03/04/87)

Drinking is thought to be more dangerous if you are a woman. A report in July 1987 claimed that 'three glasses of wine can double a woman's chances of getting breast cancer.'

Another (American) report found that women were two and a half times more likely to develop a malignant breast tumour 'if they drank the equivalent of one tot of spirits a day'.

Daily Express (07/05/87)

The *British Medical Journal* has warned its readers of the perils of the common cocktail stick.

Mr Christopher Rand, an orthopaedic surgeon in South London, gave details of three patients who had been accidentally punctured by cocktail sticks.

In all three cases the wounds failed to heal for weeks. Surgical investigation showed that the tips of the cocktail sticks had broken off and could not be detected even with the help of X-rays.

Independent (22/12/87)

Subsequently, the *BMJ* reported the case of a 38-year-old Birmingham man who died after a four-centimetre cocktail stick penetrated his windpipe.

Independent (16/02/88)

Ecstasy

Ecstasy, the recreational drug used by thousands of teenagers, may cause irreversible brain damage and

chronic depression, according to Richard Green, Professor of Pharmacology, and Guy Goodwin, professor of Psychiatry, writing in the *British Medical Journal*.
Times (14/06/96)

Eggs

In a twenty-year study of 20,000 doctors, US researchers found that eating seven or more eggs per week was associated with a 23 per cent greater risk of premature death.
Daily Mail (15/04/08)

Electric Blankets

Some experts have expressed concern about the possible danger caused by electric devices such as the above. The Central Electricity Generating Board investigated the effects of the 'magnetic field' that surrounds electrical installations.

There was 'uncertainty' about the effects an electric blanket could have on a couple's love life or whether it might increase the risk of birth defects.
Independent (18/03/88)

Electric blankets can be deadly, according to scientists at Wayne State University in Michigan. Women who used the blankets for twenty years or more were found to be 36 per cent more likely to

develop cancer of the womb.
Daily Mail (26/12/07)

Emails

Scientists from Glasgow and Paisley Universities
report that employees are becoming tired, frustrated
and unproductive as a result of constantly monitoring
emails. Females, they claimed, were most at risk.
Observer (12/08/07)

Firelighting

Don't burn colour newsprint in the fireplace. Lead in the inks can be released into the room in levels dangerous to children.

Mail on Sunday (18/11/84)

Fishing

Fishing, thought to be a peaceful activity, is in fact one of the most dangerous sports, according to figures issued by the Office of Population Censuses and Surveys. More fishermen die than those engaged in motorcycle sports, it was claimed.

Daily Telegraph (14/12/88)

Fizzy Drinks

Professor David Wray of Glasgow Dental Hospital
warns that preservatives in fizzy drinks can cause
an allergic reaction which results in chronic
inflammation of the lips, gums and face and
'a cobblestone texture on the inside of the mouth'.

The conditions can also be caused by drinking
milk, the professor claims.

The Week (29/08/98)

Flip-flops

Wearing flip-flops can put people at risk of developing
skin cancer, warned Anthony Kontos, a podiatric
surgeon at the hospital of Sir John and St Elisabeth.

Daily Telegraph (13/06/08)

Fly Sprays

Beware the deadly fly spray says the *European Journal
of Cancer*.

Using chemicals to kills flies, ants or wasps, says a
study, can trigger the growth of skin cancer.

Daily Mail (06/04/07)

Foxes

Urban foxes, currently gaining in numbers, pose a serious threat to small children. Their excrement carries thousands of minute eggs which can infect humans and even result in blindness, says Dr John Lewis, a London University biologist.
Daily Telegraph (13/08/88)

Fruit juice

Too many sugary drinks and fruit juices substantially increase the risk of gout, according to a report published in the *British Medical Journal*.
Daily Telegraph (01/02/08

Gardening

Gardening, widely thought of as a peaceful pastime, is, in fact, fraught with risks.

Any gardener, or would-be gardener, should consider the following:

A scientist in Birmingham unearthed the most conclusive evidence to date that people who grow their own vegetables in or near British cities are at risk from cadmium poisoning which can cause kidney damage.
The Times (10/10/84)

In August 1986, a health official warned that gardeners who used knapsack-style sprayers to keep

bugs at bay run a risk of poisoning themselves.
Daily Telegraph (20/08/86)

In 1981 alone, more than 3,300 people received hospital treatment for injuries inflicted by powered lawnmowers.
Daily Express (26/3/84)

Other power tools are equally dangerous.

Strimmer rash is a term used by doctors to describe a new form of dermatitis. The rash is caused by plant substances called psoralens which can be sprayed on to the skin of anyone using a strimmer and which damage the skin when exposed to the ultra-violet rays of the sun.
The Times (30/07/86)

In June 1987 a report by the Consumers Association warned that gardening could lead to swollen joints, rashes, tender skin, breathing difficulties and sickness.
Almost a quarter of gardeners questioned developed allergic reactions to plants.

Rue Blister Shock
A three-year-old girl developed blisters and had to spend a week in hospital after crawling through a bed of rue.

Primula Peril

A woman who dead-headed a neighbour's primula developed a painful rash and the skin on her hands peeled off like a pair of gloves.

Deadly Daffodils

Other plants which caused rashes, itching and swelling included:

> courgettes
> daffodils
> hyacinths
> tomatoes
> strawberries

Sap Horror

Chemicals in the sap of some plants can cause soreness or itching.

The humble geranium can prompt hay-fever-type symptoms.

Runner beans can result in a rash.

Daily Telegraph (09/06/87)

4,000 feet per annum are pierced by garden forks, according to a report published by the Consumers Association in October 1987.

Guardian (22/10/87)

Global Warming

Rising temperatures caused by global warming could lead to 'substantial increases' in cases of skin cancer, warned Dutch researcher Dr Jan van der Leun of energy consultants, Ecofys.

Metro (21/04/08)

Gold Teeth

An American dental journal, the *Probe*, has identified a phenomenon known as dental mugging. Visitors to New York who have gold fillings should beware of muggers who are liable to throw their victims to the ground and wrench out their gold caps.

Daily Express (06/08/87)

Grapefruit

The *British Journal of Cancer* has reported that eating grapefruit can increase the risk of breast cancer among post-menopausal women by almost a third.

Daily Mail (16/07/07)

Hair dye

A study conducted in six European countries has found that women who dye their hair have a higher chance of developing cancers of the lymph system and leukaemia.

Sunday Times (11/06/06)

Have a Nice Day

Sandi Mann, a psychologist at Salford University, has warned of the dangers of forced cheerfulness amongst sales staff. 'Having to hide how you really feel and fake enthusiasm to customers who are rude to you can cause hypertension, coronary heart disease and can even exacerbate cancer,' she said.

The Week (17/01/98)

Herbs

In October 1983, Dr Raymond Penn, principal medical officer at the Department of Health, warned of the health risks involved in taking a number of herbal favourites.

Mistletoe

This is used to lower blood pressure and sometimes to fight cancer. But it can cause liver damage.

Liquorice

This can cause high blood pressure.

Ginseng

According to Dr Penn, long-term use can result in victims becoming very nervous and tense. They may also develop high blood pressure. Dr Penn also warned that Asian herbal mixtures may contain substances like arsenic, mercury, tin, zinc or lead.

Holidays

Taking a holiday is wrongly considered to be beneficial health-wise.

In 1986 Cary Cooper, Professor of Organisational Psychology at the University of Manchester's Institute of Science and Technology, drew attention to the 'increasing evidence that holidays can cause harmful stress rather than provide welcome rest and reinvigoration.'

The Professor maintained that the most smooth-running holiday produces stress simply by being a change in routine.

Sunday Times (31/08/86)

Professor Cooper's findings were confirmed by a MORI poll conducted for GIS Leisure-care which found that only four in a hundred holiday-makers are carefree. Almost all of those questioned said they worry more on holiday than they do at home. Four out of ten holiday-makers worried about their homes being broken into while they were away. More than a quarter feared they would be upset by rowdy holiday-makers and 22 per cent had nightmares about being mugged.

Daily Mail (22/02/88)

Sunbathing is highly dangerous (see **sunshine**).

Sex at siesta time is a major hazard. In September

1986 a hospital consultant in Majorca warned holiday-making Britons of the dangers of attempting sexual intercourse during the heat of the afternoon. The result could be a heart attack, he warned.
Daily Mail (01/09/86)

Sightseeing is dangerous, according to doctors in Florence. After researching the subject for three years they identified a new illness which affects tourists, 'particularly middle-aged women who live monotonous lives'.

A surfeit of culture produces a 'racing heart, breathlessness, buzzing ears, trembling and anguish indicating a loss of identity.'
Daily Telegraph (05/06/86)

Another hazard was identified in a newspaper report in 1987 – falling off balconies.

The *Daily Express* claimed that railings on foreign balconies were 'far too low for safety by British standards.' According to the report, five patients in Yorkshire and more in other parts of the country will never walk again following spinal injuries after toppling from their balconies abroad.
Daily Express (23/04/87)

Sandflies are only one of many dangers lurking on the beaches of the Mediterranean.

Scientists have discovered that the bite of a sandfly can transmit a disease known as visceral

leishmaniasis which can prove fatal. In July 1987 Mr Cyril Pugh returned from a holiday in Benidorm and was admitted to hospital suffering from flu-type symptoms. Eleven days later he was dead – the victim of a sandfly bite.

Guardian (22/10/87)

Home

Writing in the authoritative magazine *Scientific American*, Dr Anthony Nero has warned that the average home may be the source of many varied forms of pollution.

Dr Nero said that cooking appliances that burn natural gas, oil or wood may also emit trace organic chemicals, carbon oxides and nitrogen oxides. Bacteria and fungi also contributed towards pollution. 'Most of these can lead to chronic or acute diseases such as respiratory infections and allergic responses,' he said.

Daily Telegraph (18/04/88)

Home Insulation

A leading building surveyor warned in June 1983 of the threat to health posed by modern heating and insulation methods. Mr Malcolm Hollis claimed that lack of ventilation led to a growing degree of radiation poisoning, resulting in more than 1,500 deaths per year.

The Times (23/05/83)

Hospitals

Many people think of hospitals as places where they become healthier. Not so. Readers are advised to avoid going to hospital if they can. The risks are considerable.

Mr Trevor Clay, Secretary of the Royal College of Nursing, revealed that hospitals were more dangerous than ever for patients.

'They contain sicker people, more complicated drugs and equipment and the risk of cross infection is always present,' he said.

The Times (07/05/87)

In 1983, the Public Health Laboratory Service reported that the organism which causes the pneumonia Legionnaires' Disease was commonly found in British hospitals.

The Times (09/12/83)

It was reported in December 1987 that about 1,000 people die every year in Britain because of mistakes by surgeons. The misdirected enthusiasm of junior doctors was blamed for unnecessary operations and occasional deaths, said the Confidential Enquiry into Perioperative Deaths published by the Nuffield Provincial Hospitals Trust.

Independent (09/12/87)

According to National Statistics, UK deaths from the superbug MRSA totalled 1,652 in 2006. Statistics also show that Clostridium Difficile infects 50,000

patients a year. 6,480 death certificates listed
C. Difficile in 2006.
Daily Mail (22/05/08)

Researchers from the Wellcome Trust and Bristol
University warned of a new hospital superbug
Stenotrophomonas maltophilia (Steno). In 2007 there
were 1,000 cases of blood poisoning caused by Steno,
of which 300 were fatal.
Guardian (07/05/08)

Housework
Men should avoid giving up jobs in order to devote
increased time to housework, said a group of
scientists in Wisconsin. Defying conventional sexual
stereotypes can give rise to stress leading to illness
and premature death.
The Week (28/12/02)

Infidelity
Dr Robert de Vito, chairman of the Psychiatry
Department at Loyola University's School of
Medicine, warns that keeping a secret from your
partner can create a variety of physical and
psychiatric ailments ranging from vomiting to
psychotic mental disorders.
Daily Mail (30/08/88)

Japanese Restaurants

A 63-year-old New Yorker became confused and pale after eating wasabi (a powerful horseradish) in a Japanese restaurant. He began to sweat heavily, staggered from the restaurant and collapsed on the pavement outside.

Writing in the *Journal of the American Medical Association* his doctor warned that people at risk from heart attacks or strokes should be careful when eating wasabi for the first time.

Independent (12/01/88)

Joss Sticks

Joss sticks and the incense used in churches are dangerous, say researchers from Taiwan and the USA. Experts found that gases in the smoke include carbon monoxide, nitrogen dioxide, sulphur dioxide and volatile organic compounds – linked to headaches, lung disorders, cancer liver damage and nerve problems.

Metro (12/05/08)

Keeping Fit

Attempting to keep fit is fraught with danger.

Squash

Squash players have a higher chance of a heart attack than participants in other energetic sports, according

to the *British Heart Journal*.
The Times (11/10/83)

Aerobics
In March 1983 an expert warned that 'fitness hopefuls can seriously damage their health with aerobics'.
Daily Mail (01/03/84)

Slimming
Slimming, particularly if there is too sudden a weight loss, if the diet is unbalanced, or if either of these factors is associated with sudden severe exercise, can occasionally be fatal.
The Times (13/09/85)

Jogging
In a study of the deaths of thirty joggers who ran between seven and a 105 miles a week, nineteen died while jogging, six died suddenly immediately afterwards, and two were found dead in bed.
The Times (15/09/84)

Dr Roger McCarter, 'a specialist in ageing research' at the University of Texas in San Antonio, is working on the theory that exercise may be extremely dangerous.

Dr McCarter believes that each human being may be allocated a limited amount of calories to burn during a lifetime.

Says the doctor: 'If you use those calories quickly by having a high metabolic rate such as one has while

exercising, then it could shorten your lifespan.
Sunday Telegraph (21/02/88)

Keyboards

Computer keyboards can harbour more harmful
bacteria than a lavatory seat, says a scientific survey
conducted by *Which?* magazine.
Daily Mail (01/05/08)

Kitchens

Kitchens are known to be especially dangerous places.
Here are a few things to watch out for:

Aluminium Pots and Pans

These produce soluble compounds when acid water
and/or acid foods (like fruit) are heated.
Sunday Telegraph (20/09/87)

According to a report in the *Independent* (18/11/86),
it is unwise to defrost food in an oven because of
the risks of food poisoning. Parts of the defrosting
food will hover between 20°c and 40°c – the perfect
range for bacteria. Dr David Southgate, head of
the food quality division at the Food Research
Institute, Norwich, has pointed out that bacteria
produce toxins which are as dangerous to humans
as microbes.

Microwave Ovens
These can cause certain foods, like eggs, to explode.
In May 1987, a steak and kidney pudding exploded in
Bedford when the cook plunged a serving spoon into
the pastry. She suffered burns to her neck, face and
hands and had to be treated in hospital.
Daily Express (21/05/87)

Household cleaning fluids carry hidden dangers. Three
women suffered breathing problems after they mixed
household ammonia with domestic bleach.
The Times (23/05/86)

Laptops

Laptops are bad for men's sperm, according to
researchers at New York State University. Men who
frequently place computers on their laps are damaging
their fertility, they warn.

Daily Mail (26/12/07)

Left-handed, dangers of being

A neurologist at Glasgow University, Dr Peter Behan,
has shown a link between left-handed people and a
variety of distressing conditions.

According to the doctor, left-handedness (or having
a left-handed mother) is closely associated with
epilepsy, congenital heart disease, severe migraine,
allergic disorders, dyslexia (twelve times more
common in left-handed people), childhood stuttering,
the hyperkinetic syndrome and autism.

The Times (21/12/84)

Light Bulbs

Low-energy light bulbs can trigger epilepsy, a
Government minister has admitted. Sufferers from
lupus, an auto-immune disease, may also be affected.

Daily Mail (25/06/07)

Mackerel Peril

Housewives should avoid buying mackerel as it can

cause poisoning, causing itching and burning of the
skin, severe headache, vomiting and diarrhoea.
The Times (07/01/87)

Marathon running

Running the marathon is fraught with hazards:

Armpits – they can become extremely sore as a
result of chafing from repetitive motion.

Nipples – these have been known to bleed after
hours in a synthetic vest.

Heart – one in 50,000 runners has a heart attack.

Mouth – over-hydration can cause runners to
collapse and even die.

Toenails – some runners find whole toenails falling
out of their socks at the end of the race.

Independent on Sunday (06/04/08)

Margarine

Scientists working on the European Community
Multicentre Study on Antioxidants, Myocardial
Infarction and Breast Cancer have warned that
margarine can cause breast cancer in women aged
between 50 and 74.

The Week (13/09/97)

Mascara

Experts at the College of Optometrists have warned of

the dangers when women apply mascara in a hurry.

A report advises 'scratching the eye with a mascara wand is the most common injury from make-up and can lead to eye infections.'

Mascara kept beyond its 'use-by date' can lead to itchy, watery and red eyes, added leading optometrist Dr Susan Blakeney.
Daily Mail (04/06/07)

Meat

In a book called *Why You Don't Need Meat* (Thorsons, 1986) author Peter Cox writes as follows: 'In 1981 a massive statistical world survey of 41 countries (including the US and the UK) was completed. The results confirm the connection between eating meat and the risks of certain types of cancer.'

Melons

Melons have been found to be a source of viral gastroenteritis on a number of occasions.
Independent (13/10/87)

Milk

Drinking a pint of skimmed milk a day increases the risk of acne by 50 per cent, reports the Harvard School of Public Health.
Daily Mail (09/05/07)

Mobile Phones

Mobiles can seriously damage the heart and kidneys, claims Professor Edward Tuddenham, a haematologist at the Imperial College Medical School.
Daily Mail (13/12/99)

Long-term mobile phone users have nearly double the risk of getting a tumour on a nerve connecting the ear to the brain, say scientists at the Karoliuska Institute in Stockholm.
Daily Telegraph (14/10/04)

A research project conducted by Dr Alan Preece at Bristol University is expected to show that exposure to mobile phone radiation affects short-term ability to perform simple mental tasks.
Sunday Times (20/12/98)

A study of 11,000 mobile phone users by Dr Kjell-Hansson Mild at the National Institute of Working Life in Umea, Sweden, suggested an increase in fatigue, headaches and skin irritation in regular users.
Sunday Times (20/12/98)

Scientists at Lund University, Sweden, found that two minutes of exposure to emissions from mobile phones can cause proteins and toxins to leak into the brain, so increasing the chances of developing Alzheimer's, multiple sclerosis and Parkinson's.
Daily Mail (13/12/99)

Radio waves from mobile phones damage DNA, in some cases irreparably, a four-year EU-funded study concluded.
The Week (08/01/05)

Pregnant women who use mobiles are more likely to have children with behavioural problems, according to researchers from the universities of California and Los Angeles (UCLA) writing in the *Journal of Epidemiology*.
Independent on Sunday (18/05/08)

However, being without a mobile can be a source of great stress. Experts working for the post office identified a condition they called 'nomophobia'. 'Being phoneless can bring on a panicky symptom in our 24/7 culture,' said telecom expert Stewart Fox-Mills.
Daily Mail (31/03/08)

Mould Madness

Mould in houses can cause allergic reactions for between ten and twenty per cent of the population and can cause mental illness, according to environmental health experts.
The Times (11/10/85)

Museums

Visiting museums is fraught with danger, according to *MAG*, the London museums and galleries magazine. Many people fail to realise the amount of walking that may be involved. They are advised to pack a bottle of water and do warm-up exercises before they start.

The Week (02/11/96)

Music

Playing or learning a musical instrument may seem a relatively safe occupation. Beginners, however, may like to bear the following in mind before embarking on a career as a musician.

Bagpipes
A fungal infection known as crytococcus neoformans can fester inside a bagpipe bag and spread to the player's lungs.

Flute
A condition known as 'flautists' chin' is an unpleasant softening of the skin caused by a fungus which flourishes on dribblers.
Evening Standard (07/07/86)

Violin
A report by Hunter Fry in the *Lancet* (September 1986) identified a condition known as 'violinists' neck', caused by long hours holding the instrument between chin and shoulder.

Cello
Cellists, according to the *Lancet* report, are especially prone to pains in the lower part of the back.

Horns, Trumpets, etc.
Musicians rash enough to play these instruments run the risk of near black-outs when playing sustained

high notes. Both the trumpet and the oboe, being high-pressure instruments, may aggravate such conditions as hernias and piles.

Percussion
Marginally safer. Even so, percussionists can suffer damage to the neck, hands and joints. There is even a variation known as cymbal-player's shoulder.
Lancet (September 1986)

Nappies
Wolfgang Kippel, a scientist at the University of Kiel, blames disposable nappies for the increase in male infertility in Western Europe. The nappies, he claims, heat up baby boys' testicles and prevent them from developing normally.
The Week (23/12/00)

Nasty Boss, A
An unpleasant boss can lead to the increased risk of heart disease. A group of employees in a healthcare institute registered a dramatic leap in blood pressure when working for a boss they dreaded.
The Week (28/12/02)

Non-stick pans
A potentially dangerous chemical, perfluorooctanoic

acid (PFOA), which is used in non-stick frying pans, may retard babies' growth, according to researchers at Johns Hopkins Bloomberg School of Public Health in Baltimore, Maryland.

Independent on Sunday (26/08/07)

Octopi

Doctors writing in the *British Medical Journal* have drawn attention to the dangers of the 'octopus', an elastic strap with metal hooks used to secure luggage on the roof rack of a car.

They point out that the Bristol Eye Hospital has recently treated six people for injuries caused by one of these perilous devices. One patient's eye was damaged by shards from his spectacle lenses. Four others had their eyesight permanently affected.

Independent

Offices

Offices constitute a major health hazard, as the following facts reveal: eighty per cent of office workers blame their illnesses on their place of work, according to a survey by the Health Promotions Research Trust. The perils include:

Building Sickness
Especially prone to affect those working in air-conditioned offices.

Lethargy
Followed by stuffy noses, dry throats, dry or itching
eyes and headaches.
Daily Telegraph (20/5/87)

An American firm, ACVA Atlantic, published a report
claiming that half of British office buildings could
pose health hazards for their staff.

The report claimed that dirty air-conditioning
systems and inadequate ventilation resulted in
fungi and bacteria being introduced into the office
atmosphere.

Mr Gary Robertson, President of ACVA Atlantic,
said: 'We already know that dirty air-conditioning is a
significant health hazard. The first fatal epidemic of
Legionnaires' Disease was traced to bacteria growing
in a dirty air-conditioning system.

'Lesser outbreaks of colds or flu-like illnesses
often occur in the workplace, but the source is rarely
identified. In many cases, it is the building itself.'
Daily Telegraph (27/01/88)

The office telephone is also a major source of illness,
according to a brochure issued by Phonotas.

'There is probably no greater focal point of
infection than the office telephone,' says the
brochure. 'The pathogenic bacteria transferred
through infected telephones are mainly staphylococci
and streptococci, although yeasts and influenza
viruses are sometimes present.

'Sources of infection for telephone users may be secretions of the nose, mouth and throat.'

Dr Arnold Wilkins of the Applied Psychology Unit, Cambridge, has recently identified another serious hazard of office life – fluorescent lighting.

Dr Wilkins' research shows that imperceptible flickers in tube lighting can trigger severe eye-strain, headaches and other complaints.

'We are looking at something that affects the quality of life of many people,' said Dr Wilkins.

Observer (10/01/88)

(See also **computers** and **desks**)

Oily Fish

Often commended as a health-giving food, oily fish are in fact dangerous, according to *New Scientist* magazine. The flesh of the fish has been found to contain dangerous chemicals which can cause diabetes.

*Daily Mail (12/04/07_*

Oral Sex

American scientists writing in the *New England Journal of Medicine* state that performing oral sex can increase the risk of throat cancer.

The Times (10/5/07)

Oranges and Lemons

Oranges are popularly considered to be good for you. But a report in the *Guardian* quoted a medical report to the effect that people who eat large amounts of citrus fruits run the risk of turning orange.

Guardian (19/01/84)

In June 1985 the Liberal MP, Mr Simon Hughes, said that the lemon was dangerous, especially when used in gin and tonic, coca-cola, etc.

According to Mr Hughes, researchers from London University had found twenty times the recommended safety level of fungicide on the skins of lemons.

Daily Telegraph (27/06/85)

Organic Chickens

Research, commissioned by ITV's *Tonight with Trevor McDonald*, has shown that organic chickens are more likely to carry the superbug campylobacter than factory-reared birds.

Daily Mail (11/06/07)

Oysters

A report in the *Journal of the American Medical Association* reported the case of a woman who contracted ulcers after eating two dozen oysters from an oyster bed with a reputation for being 'clean'.

The *Independent* concluded: 'This sadly means that

while people who eat oysters from unapproved beds, which can easily be contaminated, are knowingly taking their lives into their own hands, people who take great care may also be unlucky.

(10/11/87)

Paint

Writing in the *Journal of Occupational Environmental Medicine*, scientists from Manchester and Sheffield Universities claimed that painters and decorators are likely to have a low sperm count.

Daily Telegraph (24/05/08)

Painting and Photography

The *Times* reported (27/04/84) that volatile organic solvents used in brush and roller cleaners can cause headaches, nausea and dizziness, fainting and chronic chest complaints.

Photographers frequently contract dermatitis from chemicals in their darkroom solutions.

Passive Smoking

Inhaling second-hand smoke for as little as half an hour damages blood vessels and can lead to heart attacks and strokes, says Dr Yerem Yeghiazarians of California University.

Metro (07/05/08)

Pen Tops

Between 1969 and 1984 eight British children
suffocated when the pen top they had been sucking
lodged in their windpipes.

An ear, nose and throat specialist, Dr David Mathias,
of the Royal Victoria Infirmary, Newcastle upon Tyne,
tested a whole range of commonly available pen tops.

'There are currently only one or two pen tops
that are relatively safe,' he said. 'The standard cheap
ballpoint pen top is potentially a disaster.'
The Times (08/08/86)

Personal Stereos

In 1983 the Association of the Hard of Hearing, the
British Deaf Association, the National Deaf Children's
Society and the Royal National Institute for the
Deaf issued a joint report warning of the dangers
of listening to personal hi-fi tape players and radios
which they claimed can cause deafness.
Morning Star (30/12/83)

Their conclusions have been confirmed by a leading
American audiologist, Dr George Haspiel, who claimed
that 22 million Americans have hearing problems,
many of them caused by personal sound systems.
Daily Mail (12/10/87)

Dr Ross Coles, deputy director of the Institute for
Hearing Research in Nottingham, has concluded that

blaring loud music through headphones can become physically addictive.

Jonathan Hazel, a consultant neurologist for the Royal National Institute for the Deaf, agreed. 'High levels of sound reduce anxiety and help take away inhibitions,' he said. 'It is similar to alcohol in that the sound causes initial excitement and then has a sedative effect.'

Pets

Most domestic pets are known to be dangerous. Here are a few of the hazards involved, which you should bear in mind before acquiring a pet of any kind.

Dogs

Two doctors at Manchester University's Department of Medicine reported in September 1984 that dogs are 'a major cause of the spread of disease and infection in human beings'.

Doctors David Baxter and Professor Ian Lack claimed that dogs are responsible for over 70,000 cases of infection in humans every year.

Daily Telegraph (05/09/84)

In January 1987 the *British Medical Journal* reported that there is a relationship between a severe form of gastroenteritis in children and the presence of a dog, very often a young puppy, in the household.

The Times (23/01/87)

The Government's senior veterinary officer, Dr Fred Landeg, has advised pet owners not to let dogs sleep on their bed or even in their bedroom. Apart from the risk of unknown toxic diseases, dogs also carry common food poisoning bugs (campylbacteria and salmonella) and are also thought to carry the superbug MRSA.
The Times (21/04/08)

If you insist on owning a cat or a dog, refrain from kissing them. According to the *Daily Mail* (06/12/86), you could catch a bacterial infection which could result in meningitis.

Tropical Fish

These seem innocuous enough. But cleaning out the
fish tank by hand can result in a skin problem known
as 'fish-tank granuloma'. The problem manifests itself
as red, painful pus-filled lumps and is caused when
Mycobacterium marinum infects the broken skin.
The Times (18/10/85)

Pet Birds

Last year a Dutch medical team claimed that budgies
rival cigarettes as a cause of lung cancer.

Dr Peter Holst said that his research showed that
people with pet birds were eight times more prone to
developing lung cancer than those without them.
Daily Telegraph (12/06/87)

Psittacosis is also common among bird fanciers.
The disease may present itself as a mild flu-like
illness with a cough, aches and pains, headaches and
sore throat. But in more severe cases an associated
pneumonia develops, or there may be complications
due to the spreading of the infection to the heart or
lining of the brain.
The Times (14/09/84)

That pigeon-fancying is highly dangerous is shown by
the following incident.

In December 1986 an inquest was told that a Mr
Hector Connolly died from Pigeon Fancier's Lung,
an allergic disease caused by the inhalation of protein

dust from birds, feathers or their droppings. (Mr Connolly's case, it was reported, was typical. He had been breeding pigeons for forty years and always kept them meticulously clean.)

The Times (19/12/86)

Cats

It is a mistake to think that the common cat flea is harmless, according to a report in the *Times*.

A leading authority on fleas, Dr Bernice Williams, of the Medical Ectomology Centre at Cambridge University claims that the flea's ability to carry and transmit disease has been severely underestimated.

She says the flea can also pass on the rodent diseases of bubonic plague and marine typhus from injected animals to humans.

The Times (04/08/86.)

Another report has recently warned of the danger of being scratched by your cat. This can lead to cat-scratch disease. The symptoms are 'swollen glands in the head, neck or armpits, fever and feeling out of sorts.'

Diagnosis can only be confirmed by a special skin test. The disease ought to be suspected when a lump appears where the claws have damaged the skin and if there are swollen lymph glands in the same part of the body.

Independent (18/11/86)

Toxoplasmosis, a condition with symptoms similar to those of glandular fever, is spread by cats who catch it from eating mice.

Fifty per cent of British people are infected with the protozoa *Toxoplasma gondii* at some time, according to the distinguished medical expert Dr Thomas Stuttaford.

The Times (04/02/88)

Dr Stuart Copperman of New York State spent sixteen years researching cat-related ailments. He concluded that in addition to unusual complaints such as 'cat-scratch' disease and toxoplasmosis, cats were also responsible for recurrent throat infections.

In scores of cases Dr Copperman traced the infection to a cat carrying streptococcal bacteria.

Independent (22/09/87)

Rabbits

The Health Protection Agency has warned that Rabbit Flu is the most common disease to spread from animal to humans.

Guardian (21/08/06)

Playgrounds

A superbug known as Panton-Velentine Leukocidia (PVL) is on the rise in Britain's playgrounds and is capable of killing children in one to two days. The warning comes from Richard Wise, Professor of Molecular Epidemiology at Imperial College, London.

Daily Telegraph (28/04/08)

Politics

Becoming an MP has been found to be fraught with danger. A study of politicians by Ashley Weinberger of Salford University revealed that within months of being elected, MPs were suffering from anxiety and feelings of inadequacy. After a year, a third of those questioned were found to suffer from insomnia, chest pains and dizzy spells. Many had taken to drink.

The Week (23/12/00)

Popcorn

Popcorn, a favourite snack of millions of Americans, can cause a potentially fatal health condition known as 'popcorn makers' lung,' says food consultant Dr Cecil Rose.

Independent (06/09/07)

Potato Skins

Research at Cornell University has shown that too many potato skins can damage your health.

Independent (06/07/87)

Pot Plants

A study published in *Occupational and Environmental Medicine* claims that using pesticides on house plants can double the risk of developing a brain tumour.

Daily Mail (05/06/07)

Poultry

Intensive methods of poultry and cattle rearing have
resulted in the majority of poultry carcases and a large
proportion of beef being contaminated at the abattoir
by faeces from symptomless carriers of salmonella.

The Times (14/09/84)

Queueing

Dr Terry Looker, deputy head of biological sciences at
Manchester Polytechnic, has claimed that people who
become angry when confronted by queues (or faulty
telephone boxes) are running the risk of an early death.

Says Dr Looker: 'They get angry, their heart rate and blood pressure increases and they undergo the physiological changes one would have when fighting a sabre-toothed tiger. It may sound far-fetched, but these things can cause a heart attack. There should be a Government health warning on the "Queue Here" sign at a Post Office.'

Daily Telegraph (08/02/88)

Raw Eggs

The Department of Health has warned people not to eat raw eggs or uncooked foods made with them, such as mayonnaise. There is mounting evidence that they can lead to food poisoning, it was claimed.

Daily Telegraph (27/08/88)

Rice

Rice used to be thought of as an innocuous part of any Chinese or Indian meal, but recently research workers linked polished rice with duodenal ulceration.

The Times (11/06/87)

Salt

The National Advisory Committee on Nutrition Education has linked high consumption of salt with raised blood pressure, a major factor in the development of heart disease.

Daily Telegraph (12/10/83)

According to the *Daily Express* (11/06/87) taking too much salt with one's meal could also be a major factor in triggering asthma attacks.

Sausages

Dr Justin Stebbin of St George's Hospital, London, has discovered that sausages contain nitrates which in excess can have a devastating effect on the blood. The doctor instances the case of a 58-year-old man who ate ten sausages in twenty minutes and who nearly died following a dramatic drop of blood pressure.
The Week (13/12/97)

The World Cancer Research Fund has warned that eating one sausage a day can increase the risk of bowel cancer by twenty per cent. The same applies to all processed meat (bacon, ham, hot dogs, etc.)
'We recommend that people avoid them altogether,' said Professor Martin Wiseman.
Daily Mail (31/03/08)

September 6th

Researchers working for the chemist chain Lloyd's Pharmacy have identified September 6th as the day on which most Britons are likely to fall ill.
Daily Mail (06/09/07)

Sex

Readers will not be surprised to learn that this is fraught with danger.

In young women it can lead to cancer of the cervix. In March 1984 a cancer specialist advised women to refrain from sexual intercourse until they were in their twenties to lower the chance of contracting this cancer.
The Times (16/03/84)

Professor Jean-Paul Brouster of Bordeaux University has claimed that sex can lead to a heart attack.
The Professor says: 'At around fifty, having sex with your wife is like climbing three floors or taking a three-and-a-half mile walk in the country.
'But with a girlfriend it is like racing up the stairs of a skyscraper or sprinting five miles.'
Daily Express (18/01/84)

Another expert, Mr Stephen Sadler of the British School of Osteopathy, has concluded that sex can seriously damage your back. 'Even getting in and out of bed or going to the loo can bring on acute attacks of back pain,' he said.
Daily Express (25/05/87)

A report in the *Independent* (18/11/86) claimed that 'people can develop headaches during sexual intercourse.'
(See also **Holidays**)

Another report, published in August 1987 by medical

researchers Andrew Keat and Josh Dixey, established a link between sex and arthritis. An estimated 10,000 new cases each year are thought to be victims of SARA (Sexually Acquired Reactive Arthritis).
Sun (12/08/87)

A leading ear nose and throat surgeon, Mr Ian Mackay, has discovered that sexual arousal in men stimulates mucous secretions in the nose which then becomes blocked. One of his patients complained that he couldn't stop sneezing after sexual intercourse.
Marie Claire magazine (July 89)

Sitting Down

Professor Marc Hamilton of the University of Missouri has warned that workers who sit at desks all day and then go home to sit in front of the TV run the risk of heart disease, type 2 diabetes and obesity.
Daily Mail (09/11/07)

Skating

'Ice rinks,' says a report, 'provide a steady stream of visitors to local hospitals.' In the first six months after the opening of an ice rink near the Ulster Hospital in County Down, 636 people injured themselves. The youngest was five and the oldest was 81. Most injuries are to the knees and head.
Independent (12/01/88)

Sleeping

This involves a number of risks.

According to an advertisement issued by Dunlopillo, the average human being loses a pint and a half of body fluid every night through evaporation from the skin pores. A damp mattress which absorbs moisture 'creates ideal breeding conditions for bacteria.'

Changing to a waterbed will not ensure nocturnal safety. In 1987 a research team from the University of Rochester, New York, found that the position adopted while sleeping on a waterbed was associated with heartburn. Of a group of fifty sufferers of oesophageal reflex, nine had waterbeds.

An after-dinner nap is widely considered to be an aid to digestion. But in April 1984, Dr Tom de Meester told an International Doctors Conference in Florence that this was a mistaken belief.

Said the doctor, 'After a good meal it is better not to nap, smoke, drink, worry – or worse – make love. All of them can be the cause of bad digestion resulting in ulcers.'
Sunday Express (08/04/84)

While hot water bottles cannot give you deadly diseases, they can be responsible for a nasty bout of chilblains.
Independent (27/01/87)
(See also Electric Blankets)

Smiling

A leading Japanese psychiatrist has warned women working in the convenience store industry of the dangers of smiling. All-day smiling can lead to depression, he says, in addition to painful muscles and headaches.
The Times (09/02/08)

Smoking

Readers will be aware of the risks that may ensue from indulging in this pernicious vice.

According to the Health Education Council (March 1984): 'Smoking is a major cause of heart disease in this country. And even if you escape heart attacks, there is emphysema or lung cancer to worry about. Each week about 2,000 people die of smoking-related diseases.'

Smoking is also linked to:

Impotence
Studies by French doctors published in March 1985 established a link between poor blood circulation brought on in middle age by smoking.
Sunday Times (March 85)

Ulcers
Researchers writing in the *New England Journal of Medicine* claimed that smoking is the most important single cause of recurring ulcers.
Daily Telegraph (14/09/84)

Excessive Hairiness
The American magazine *Pulse* has warned women over thirty that smoking more than twenty cigarettes a day doubles their chances of developing masculine facial hair.
Mail on Sunday (09/08/87)
(See also **Smoking, Giving Up**)

Hair loss
Smoking can lead to hair loss, according to a study carried out in Taiwan in 2007. It is also linked to premature greying.
Daily Mail (27/05/08)

Deafness
Smoking, which leads to decreased oxygen flow to the brain, can also cause deafness, experts from the University of Antwerp have discovered.
Independent (10/06/08)

Smoking, Giving Up

The dangers of smoking are now well known (see **Smoking**). But it is perhaps not so widely appreciated that giving up smoking is no guarantee of good health.

Mr Martin Jarvis, a clinical psychologist at the Addiction Research Unit of the Institute of Psychiatry at the University of London, has warned that people who give up smoking may suffer from indigestion, constipation or diarrhoea.

'The evidence is building up to suggest that most people suffer quite a range of adverse effects, physiological and psychological,' he said.
The Times (April 1984)

Another report in the *Times* quoted doctors to the effect that 'people who give up smoking still run a considerable risk of suffering a heart attack.'

The research was based on a study of 7,735 middle-aged men in 24 towns who took part in the British Regional Heart study during the previous six years.
The Times (13/12/86)

In November 1986 a pathologist in Preston, Lancs, blamed the death of a thirty-year-old woman on giving up smoking.

She suffered acute withdrawal symptoms of nervous tension and shaking after putting out what she was determined would be her last cigarette, Dr Edmund Tapp told the inquest.
Daily Telegraph (05/11/86)

Snoring

Once tucked up in bed and fast asleep people think they are relatively safe. They overlook the possibility of snoring, which is a potentially lethal side-effect of sleep.

Olivia Timbs in the *Independent* (18/08/87) has written that many of those with snoring problems may develop circulation difficulties and heart disease. A Washington ear, nose and throat specialist, Dr

David Fairbanks, wrote in 1984 that snoring was a major cause of divorce and that in its most serious form, Apnea (Greek for not breathing), it can be fatal.
Sunday Express (05/02/84)

A further investigation conducted by Canadian researchers showed that habitual snorers were twice as likely as non-snorers to be involved in traffic accidents.
Lancet (September 87)

Soap

Scientists at the Institute of Child Health at University College, London, have warned that strong soaps can remove vital skin oils, thus allowing allergens and other proteins to penetrate the skin.
Daily Mail (14/06/07)

Soap Operas

A survey of 200 GPs by Norwich Union Healthcare found that two thirds of them blamed TV soaps for making their patients paranoid and reporting symptoms they had seen on the screen.
BBC News (21/04/05)

Soya

The US Food and Drug Administration has warned that this well-known health food contains chemicals

and can increase the risk of cancer in women, brain
damage in men and abnormalities in infants.
The Week (23/12/00)

Spectator Sports

Dutch scientists have warned that tension experienced
by football fans when watching penalty shoot-outs can
trigger heart attacks and strokes. On the day Holland
lost to France in a shoot-out in Euro '96, deaths
among men from these causes rose by fifty per cent.
The Week (22/12/01)

Stairs

In America 2.6 million people are injured every year

climbing or descending stairs. In Britain the figure
is 190,000.
Daily Telegraph (26/08/88)

Sugar

Research in Adelaide reported in the *British Medical
Journal* shows that heavy sugar intake increases the
chance of developing gallstones.
The Times (25/05/84)

Sunbathing

Once thought of as beneficial, sunbathing is now
known to be extremely dangerous.

Dr Robin Russell Jones, consultant dermatologist
at London's St John's Hospital for Diseases of the Skin,
warned in the *Lancet* in August 1987 that skin cancer
was on the increase because of increased exposure to
ultra-violet rays of the sun by people on holiday.

The problem was getting worse, the doctor warned,
because the ozone layer round the earth, which filters
out most ultra-violet radiation, is being depleted by
man-made chemicals.
Daily Telegraph (22/08/87)

According to a report in the *Times* (19/12/85) the sun's
rays not only produce tanning but also depress the
body's immune system and may cause outbreaks of
recurrence of cold sores. Apart from these dangers,

excessive exposure to sunlight in hot climates can lead to the development of patches of rough, warty skin which are red or skin-coloured and known as keratoses.

The Times (18/07/86)

Sunbeds

A survey for cancer research UK claimed that young people who use sunbeds are increasing their risk of skin cancer by up to 75 per cent.

Independent (08/04/08)

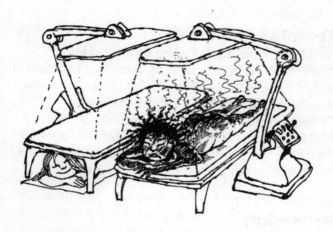

Sunglasses

Dr Sharon Moalem, described as a disease specialist, has written a book claiming that sunglasses 'can trick the brain' about harmful ultraviolet light. Said German expert Dr Sven Krengel, 'I like this theory.'

Sunday Express (03/06/07)

Talcum Powder

Women who use talcum powder 'in the pelvic area' have a higher risk of developing ovarian cancer, according to research published in the *International Journal of Cancer*.

Independent on Sunday (26/08/07)

Teetotalism

Abstaining from alcohol when young can lead to illness by the time you are forty, according to a team of scientists from the Institute of Child Health and the Australian National University in Canberra.

Teetotallers were shown to be the least healthy in a sample of 9,000 people, twice as likely to be suffering from bad physical or mental health as moderate drinkers.

The Week (26/09/98)

Television

A *Daily Mail* report in 1987 drew attention to the dangers of watching television.

Most of us slump in a favourite armchair – far too soft – heightening the risk of back strain, cramps, indigestion and damaged stomach-muscles.

Depression is another hazard because 'an unhappy person can easily use TV as an escape from the world.' In January 1984 an eleven-year-old girl lost consciousness when watching television. A spokesman at the Queen's Medical Centre in Nottingham said: 'This effect on the brain can happen to any child sitting within inches of a set.'

Professor Ivor Mills of Addenbrookes Hospital, Cambridge, made a study of the effect of violent films

on children. He commented: 'It is theoretically possible that a child could reach such a state of excitement that the heart begins to beat irregularly, blood stops circulating to the brain and the result is death.'
Daily Mail (31/01/84)

The biggest danger of viewing is to the eyes. Writing in the *Daily Mail* (13/08/87) Ian Brown says: 'While viewing won't actually cause major complaints, it will exacerbate problems that are already there and cause eye strain and headaches.'

The optical information centre has advised viewers to have soft light in the room to lessen the intensity of the screen's light on the eyes. The council also recommends that you should glance away from the set at regular intervals.

Viewers can suffer from depression when their favourite TV series ends. A survey of 1,600 viewers by the broadband firm Tiscali identified a condition called TV trauma, 'akin to a broken heart'. Among men, the most likely cause this was Billie Piper (Rose in *Dr Who*), while for women it was James Nesbitt in *Cold Feet*.
Daily Mail (28/05/08)

TV Chefs

About six million people have had accidents in their kitchens while copying TV chefs, according to a survey by the insurance company, Esure. 'A quarter of

amateurs have sliced their fingers trying to emulate the likes of Gordon Ramsay,' the report says.
Metro (24/04/08)

Tennis rackets

Tennis rackets made with nanotechnology could pose a health risk similar to asbestos, say researchers led by Ken Donaldson of Edinburgh University. Also affected are sailing ship masts, bicycles and golf clubs.
Daily Mail (21/05/08)

Toilets

These should be avoided as much as possible.

According to evidence gathered by a research team at the University of California (led by Doctors Trudy Larson and Yvonne Bryson), the genital herpes virus can survive for up to fours hours on a toilet seat.

Other tests have revealed that the organisms for cystitis, *trichonormus vaginilis*, syphilis and gonorrhoea can also survive on the surface of a toilet seat for several hours, as well as those responsible for ringworm and scabies. Similarly, the larger parasites, including pinworms, head lice and the crab louse, are harboured on the surfaces.
Research by Douce Shepard Associates

Travellers should beware of the vacuum-operated toilet which may anchor them to the seat or, worse, cause an extremely painful rupture.

Independent (01/05/87)

Toothbrushes

James Song, a biochemist working at Wisconsin University, claims that toothbrushes can be a major health hazard. 'Unhygienic toothbrushes,' he suggests, are linked to heart disease, stroke, arthritis and chronic infections.

Daily Mail (30/05/06)

Toothpicks

A study published in 1984 claimed that 8,000 Americans are injured every year while using toothpicks. Some swallow the toothpicks inadvertently, others puncture an eye or an ear.

Between 1979 and 1982 there were 8,176 'toothpick-related incidents' in the United States. Some cases proved fatal.

Daily Telegraph (14/08/84)

Trampolines

The Royal Society for the Prevention of Accidents reports that in 2006 11,500 children needed hospital treatment following trampoline-related accidents. Many needed surgery. *Daily Mail (26/12/07)*

Vasectomy

A study in the *British Journal of Cancer* has concluded that men who have had a vasectomy operation are four times more likely to develop cancer of the prostate.

The researchers looked at the tumour registry records of several hundred men in Los Angeles County.

Independent (15/04/88)

Vegetarianism

Research has shown that vegetarians have a low cholesterol level and so run a lesser risk of heart attacks than meat-eaters.

But in 1987 an American report showed that 'people with very low cholesterol levels ran an increased risk of contracting cancer.'

Today (10/08/87)

Vitamins

Many readers may think that vitamin pills are beneficial. But research by American doctors published in 1984 warned of disturbing side-effects among people who increase their vitamin intake.

Vitamin B6 (popular with keep-fit fanatics and athletes) has been known to cause severe neurological problems, including numbness, walking difficulties, sharp internal pains and loss of reflex.

Vitamin A has been responsible for the largest

number of poisoning cases.

Vitamin C, believed by some experts to prevent colds, has been blamed for inducing cramps and kidney stones.

Vitamin D can bring on loss of appetite, nausea, excessive thirst, mental confusion and kidney failure.

Vitamin E, recommended for alleviating everything from the ravages of old age to preventing cancer, has equally devastating effects if over-used.

Daily Mail (21/03/84)

Washing Up

A report published by the *British Journal of Industrial Medicine* has warned of the dangers of using washing-up liquid without rinsing the dishes.

Research workers under Professor Charles Grant Clark, Professor of Surgery at University College Hospital, London, have shown that adding diluted detergent to the drinking water of rats caused severe effects throughout the alimentary canal.

Daily Telegraph (18/06/84)

Wasps

Several people die every year as the result of a wasp sting.

The Times (11/11/83)

Water

Drinking water can lead to madness, it has been

claimed. Professor James Edwardson, director of the Medical Research Council's neuro-endocrinology unit in Newcastle upon Tyne, has found that aluminium is present in drinking water in many areas of Britain.

Exposure to high levels of aluminium is firmly linked to senile dementia, which affects more than 250,000 people in Britain.

The Times (14/02/86)

According to the European Commission in Brussels, British drinking water fails to conform to safety standards. The Commission has stated that in many parts of Britain there is too much nitrite in the water. Nitrite, says the *Sunday Times* (09/08/87), 'has been linked with stomach cancer and the "blue-baby" syndrome'.

Lead is also present in what many experts consider to be dangerous concentrations in some British tap water. Results of lead poisoning include lowering of intelligence, exhaustion, impotence, muscle and heart weakness, premature senility and death.

Sunday Times (20/09/87)

Drinking large quantities of water can also lead to epileptic attacks, it has been revealed. A report in the *British Medical Journal* detailed the case of a 32-year-old man who swallowed 'about a bathful' of water to relieve the symptoms of toothache. He became unconscious and doctors diagnosed a case of 'water

intoxication'. He later produced nine litres of urine in twelve hours.
Independent (05/04/88)

Wine

The Ministry of Agriculture and Fisheries has warned of the dangers of toxic lead affecting wine drinkers.

Professor Vincent Marks and Dr Andrew Taylor of the University of Surrey's biochemistry department showed that wine can seep out, react with the metal foil around the cork and deposit harmful lead salts on the neck of the bottle. They concluded that persistent wine drinkers can run some risk of high lead intake.
Independent (22/12/87)

Only two large glasses of wine can raise the risk of breast cancer by more than half, according to researchers at the University of Cardiff.
Daily Mail (14/04/08)

Wind farms

Wind farms can cause epileptic fits, Professor Arnold Wilkins has warned.
Daily Mail (30/04/08)

Winter

Winter causes severe depression, psychiatrists have

discovered. A report in the *British Medical Journal* says that women in particular may suffer from a syndrome known as seasonal affective disorder (SAD), which may make them anxious, tired and uninterested in sexual intercourse. Men are also prone to the disorder, but it is about nine times more common in women.

The Times (12/12/87)

Work (too little)

The private health insurance group BUPA has identified a new form of stress caused by people not having enough work to do. So-called 'underload', when a job is insufficiently challenging, leads to sickness, inefficiency and personal problems, BUPA experts warn.

Daily Telegraph (14/09/88)

Index